Finding Mother God

Finding Mother God

POEMS TO HEAL THE WORLD

Carol Lynn Pearson

GIBBS SMITH
TO ENRICH AND INSPIRE HUMANKIND

First Edition
24 23 22 21   5 4 3

Published by
Gibbs Smith
P.O. Box 667
Layton, Utah 84041

1.800.835.4993 orders
www.gibbs-smith.com

Cover illustration by Alicia Bay Laurel
Designed by Debbie Berne
Printed and bound in China

Gibbs Smith books are printed on either recycled, 100% post-consumer waste, FSC-certified papers or on paper produced from sustainable PEFC-certified forest/controlled wood source. Learn more at www.pefc.org.

Library of Congress Control Number: 2020933576

ISBN: 978-1-4236-5668-5

To our Mother God
in all Her names

CONTENTS

AUTHOR'S NOTE

Call Her Goddess—call her Heavenly Mother—call her the Feminine Principle—we need Her. Our world suffers the pain of Her absence. This book of poems is more than poetry. It is an urgent invitation for all—women and men, people of all religions and of no religion—to welcome our Mother God back into the family, to set a place for Her at the table.

One need not be a believer to understand how our ideas of the gender of God impact the status of women. Even an atheist calls God "Him." As Catholic theologian Mary Daly famously said, "If God is male, the male is god."

Bringing back our Mother is not just cosmetic—it is cosmic. With the full participation and full honoring of the female—on earth and in heaven—we have a stronger opportunity to create justice and peace, bringing the human family closer and closer to the promised land of Partnership.

"The more than usually miserable state of the world demands that the supreme Godhead be redefined, that the repressed desire of the Western races for some practical form of goddess worship be satisfied."

—Robert Graves, mythologist

My Words

These are only poems, you know.
  They have no authority.

Except for me.

I am bound by their authority
  because I authored them.

Rather like God authored me.

God signed, sealed and delivered me
  to this world of thought
    this world of paper and pen

and sentenced me to observe.

As God's signature is upon me
  so is mine upon my words.

As God's light flows to me
  and through me

so does mine through my words
  and words are windows

and the view is stunning

and the view is
  without end.

To Our Mother

Remembering that Jesus named his Father
   from the cross and said:
      "Abba, Abba, why hast thou forsaken me?"

and remembering too that on the kibbutz I learned
   that even today children speaking Hebrew
     call their father "Abba"
       and their mother "Ema"

I am amazed to find in my balancing hands
   two balancing words
     and the first speaking of the new word is this:

"Ema, Ema, why have we forsaken thee?"

A Motherless House

(written decades ago)

I live in a Motherless house
  a broken home.

How it happened I cannot learn.

When I had words enough to ask
  "Where is my Mother?"
    no one seemed to know

and no one thought it strange
  that no one else knew either.

I live in a Motherless house.

They are good to me here
  but I find that no kindly
    patriarchal care eases the pain.

I yearn for the day
  someone will look at me and say
    "You certainly do look like your Mother."

I walk the rooms, search the closets
  look for something that might have
    belonged to Her:
      a letter, a dress, a chair.

Would She not have left a note?

I close my eyes and work to
    bring back Her touch, Her face.

Surely there must have been
    a Motherly embrace
        I can call back for comfort.

I live in a Motherless house
    Motherless and without a trace.

Who could have done this?

Who would tear an unweaned infant
    from its Mother's arms and clear the place
        of every souvenir?

I live in a Motherless house.

I lie awake and listen always for the word
    that never comes, but might.

I bury my face
    in something soft as a breast.

I am a child
    crying for my Mother in the night.

Message from Mother
(appreciation to mythologist Joseph Campbell)

For all those little gifts you gave to
   the mythologists and archaeologists
      to give to me

I thank you, Mother.

For that precious big-bellied figurine pressed
   by Paleolithic hands and the magical naked
      outline of you on the walls of caves

I thank you.

I thought I was a Motherless child
   in an always Motherless house
      and then your little surprises began to come

as did my tears, my grateful tears
   for there was your soft and ancient voice:

I am here. I am female. I am divine.

Thank you for the word "mother"
   spoken centuries before the word "father"
      for blood and baby do not lie

but testify that Mother was the First Thing
　　the power that carried and birthed the universe
　　　and all in it, the sea, the earth, the animals

the upright ones, the men and women who lived
　　in peace within Her safe cycle and gathered
　　　food to the easy sound of wind and rain:

I am here. I am female. I am divine.

I thank you, Mother, for brooding over your people
　　when the dark times came, when the invaders came
　　　the Indo-Europeans from the north

and the Semites from the desert, turning the birthing
　　upside down so Athena was born of the forehead
　　　of Zeus and Eve was born of the rib of Adam.

Their gods were male
　　and their swords were bronze
　　　and they named you Abomination

and butchered and buried you without knowing
　　they were planting you, for you are the transformer
　　　who turns a seed into a tree, the Tree of Life

who is sturdy and many and grew in all places
　　the goddess of many names that I read now
　　　on pages made from the tree that speak for the tree:

I am here. I am female. I am divine.

Athena—Ceres—Cerridwen—Demeter—Diana—
   Hathor—Inanna—Isis—Kali—Maat—Venus—
      hundreds more—shining black or ivory or red
         and each a name that points to Mother.

The past does what the past is and it is gone.
   Men are still warriors, but not all, for many understand
      that our very being turns now on our turning to our

Mother, who is ready to correct our view of heaven so that
   God Herself and God Himself, who were always One
      can join on earth to bless the confused billions.

The next step is ours, daughters of our Mother
   and did we ever think She would not uphold us
      in our essential mission?

We thank you, Mother, as now we rise
   the women with microphones in the halls of government
      the halls of justice, of media, of religion

the women penning books and scribbling poems
   the women helping women buy a goat or a sewing machine
      the women marching with signs and songs.

There is power in our words and our words are these:

We are here. We are female. We are divine.

Ask the Pope or Ask an Atheist

The maleness of God is ubiquitous
 like oxygen or sand.

That sly pronoun just pops up
 without solicitation.

Ask the Pope about the gender of the divine
 and a catechism from the year 1993 replies

"He is neither man nor woman: He is God."

Or ask even a female atheist
 "Tell me about God."

She will narrow her eyes and say
 "God? There is no God.
  He does not exist!"

Miraculous.

Even without existing
 God wears a suit and a tie.

If God Is Male

God the trunk
  His power the branches.

Season after season the stories
  and revelations fall
    ripe with pronouns:

Him, Him, His, Him
  the close ground now
    thick with Him.

Him is he.

I am she.

Many are we
  the outer ring
    of fruit that fell
      far
    from
  the
Tree.

A God Who Looks Like Me

I studied the drawings and the statues
  and the words marked "God"
    hoping to find a face that looks like me
      a female face

but they all looked like my brothers

and I love my brothers
  but it's like finding an empty stocking
    on Christmas morning and wondering why

I have not been good enough
  not good enough to look like God

but not wanting to spoil the celebration
  for my brothers who never notice.

A voice said: *Come to the grove*
  at the grove there is always
    a God who looks like you.

I went to the grove and there were
  ribboned streams that flowed and curved
    and there were trees stately in long
      green gowns that waved in the wind.

A voice said: *Come to the pool.*

I went to the pool and I
   knelt and peered into the water
      still as a mirror, still as a moon

and I saw the image of God.

There was one Face
   and then the Face became two
      like when you stare with soft vision

and one of the Faces looked like me.

She said:
It is wonderful to see you seeing me.

He said:
I am so sorry.
   It never was intended that She be erased.
      Mistakes were made.

Then She said:
Bless you for searching until you found me.
   And do forgive your brothers
      for they knew not what they did.

But I knew and I know and I weep.
   You and I are half of heaven
      and to forget that is a curse in the land.

Then He said:
 Go tell it on the mountain.

But this is only a poem, I said.

Then go read it on the mountain.

And then the two Faces became one again.

A question, if I may, I said hesitantly.
  Are you two or are you one?

The water shimmered
  and I heard a choral reading
    of soprano and tenor and smile:

We are One that is Two
and Two that are One.

How can that be?

He said:
The solitary 1 is primordial but often useless.
  Imagine that buck without the doe.
    Imagine this h2 without the o.

She added:
Or distance without time
  or the occasional essential rhyme.

Then both:
We do arithmetic differently here.

A soft and rippling laugh like a kiss
  as the Face in the pool in the grove
    disappeared.

Goodbye Goddesses

I get it.

When the great religion of monotheism
   developed on the desert scene
     and Israel's prophets and kings

felt commissioned to cleanse the tents
   and the tabernacle of the false gods
     and especially the goddesses

who had infiltrated from the surrounding nations,
   requiring that they scrub every name, every symbol
     every female whiff of lily and of rose

for the Lord our God is One
   and there is none other beside Him
     and the goddess shall be called Anathema.

Never mind that the beloved Asherah had shared
   Solomon's temple with Jahweh for 236
     of the 370 years of its existence.

It happened like unto the old English marriage
   law that states when two become one
     the one is him.

So it came to pass that Asherah and her sister goddesses
  who had done their imperfect best to mother
    the people who had called them into being

were exiled all, sent without
  meat or drink or thank you or blessing
    into the unforgiving desert to die.

Inhospitality indeed!

And thus did the House of Israel
  become a Motherless House with only
    hidden tokens and whispered memories

as in the story of Rachel in her tent with the teraphim
  under her skirts, idols stolen from her father, Laban,
    little images to remind her of the old ways

when women were honored and peace reigned
  under the goddess of Mesopotamia for whom
    she was named Rachel, Mother of the Holy Lamb.

And is this ancient narrative not like unto the story
  of a man in America around the year 1912
    who might load his family into his new Model-T

for a cross-country trip, and so enthusiastic is he
  to cover the miles that he leaves his wife
    at the service station in Pittsburgh

and when one of the sleeping children
    opens her eyes and says, "Where's Mother?"
        is not the moment worthy of

a monosyllabic and screeching

halt!

of biblical proportions.

Common Sense

I may not be the sharpest knife
   in the chandelier or the brightest bulb
      in the drawer, but

seeing the creatures out in the zoo
   and the creatures up in the blue
      and the creatures on Fifth Avenue

who are pretty equally girl and guy
   I will not buy
      the Brooklyn Bridge

nor will I buy
   a story that says the Creator
      of all the creatures including me

was one or two or three Male Beings
   never mind how potent
      their omnipotence might be.

The Case of the Disappearance
of God the Mother

My friend Monica, so beautiful, so smart
  so hungry for her Mother

was viscerally fearful that her own eternal journey
  would leave her disappeared
    just like her Mother

and I have seen tears in her eyes.

If the disappearance of the mother happened
  in my house or the house of my friend
    I would call the police
      I would shout that something
        criminal had happened.

But the disappearance of the Mother of us all
  from the House in Heaven seems to have occurred
    without much excitement, much notice even
      and so very, very long ago.

It looked to be a cold case indeed
  and when finally we petitioned the authorities
    the officers at the station were
      very reluctant to stir things up.

However, Monica and I, both smart and hungry women
  knew there was something fishy going on
    and we went over their heads

and we learned some things from documents
  hidden in dark places and we also spoke to
    some higher-ups, the very highest-ups.

And the first thing we must tell you is this:

She was never gone.

That half of God can disappear is beyond absurd
  as is the notion of separation in the House of God
    for God is Love and Love is indivisible.

And the second thing we must tell you is this:

We found Her.

We called out and She answered.
  She was at home and receiving.

Her disappearance was a sham
  a story developed by men throughout history
    men who coveted because you know
      if God is male the male is god.

She never left Her place in heaven
  or Her place on earth.
    Only Her name was stolen.

She defies dimensions and will be where She will be
  and the truth that the Kingdom of God is within
    is the clue that Monica and I followed as we searched
      and it was there that She answered.

She is within and She fills us heart and mind.

She fills the galaxies, the stars and the spaces as does He.
  She fills the chapels and temples as does He
    and the mosques and the synagogues
      and the huts and the homes.

She adores the sound of the organ and the choir
  and the bells and the chanting and the humming
    and the clapping and the praying.

She is present but not accounted for
  and the only crime committed was not
    a crime against Her but a crime

against humanity Her family, a crime
  committed by humanity Her family.

Her name was stolen
  but what's in a name?

We could eat bread if it had no name
    but it would be harder to ask for.

And how lovely it is to know that
    my daily bread bears Her aroma
        and to know that all my blessings flow
            through Her hands as well as His.

Let us welcome Her with words.
    She has missed the sound of her children's voices.
        Let us grasp Her and never let go.

The men will suddenly understand
    that the ache was for Her, the emptiness they felt
        was for Her and they never knew
            and therefore the tears.

It is our privilege to tell them.

And it is our obligation to write the story.

Let us call her Mother, Goddess, First Woman
    Eternal Comforter.

Our shouts will be joyful and our songs will celebrate
    that the Queen of Heaven also is Queen of Earth

and the family is whole once more.

Does It Matter?

If we knock at the door
  of our theology and ask for Mother
    and the doorman says, "Who?"

does it really matter
  for God's in His heaven
    all's right with the world.

If we knock at the door of etymology
  and ask for Mother, an ancient voice
    recites the kinship of words:

Mother is matter
  and matter is the basic structural
    component of the universe.

Mother is matrix
  and matrix is the field
    the web that holds.

Mother is material
  and material clothed
    you and me and the mountain.

Is it immaterial, then, the lack of knowing
  the One who materialized all?

Would Her presence in our theology
    be merely cosmetic?

Or would it be cosmic?

This I know:

While God is not in Her heaven
    not all's right with the world.

Until this matter of our Mother is settled
    the inhabitants of the earth will remain uneasy

will look at each other, women and men
    without full reverence

will feel somehow that we are
    looking at the heavens with one eye blind

will feel that the foundation of the house
    is off kilter

will know, with a deep unease
    that something—something

is the matter.

Paradigm Shift

After 359 years the Pope acknowledged
  that heretic Galileo was right and

the sun does not revolve around the earth.

How long will it take men of the earth
  to acknowledge that we heretic women are right

and the female does not revolve around the male?

For we too have scoped the heavens
  revealed the center, can testify
    of the brilliant celestial bodies, and lo!

the Heavenly Him and the Heavenly Her
  do no orbiting, no presiding, no ranking

are perfect partners in a slow dance
  so close you would observe
    that they are One.

Remembering

I am remembering Her now.

Not by sight.

I am remembering Her
  rather like the blind man
    remembers a face by his fingers.

I am remembering Her by heart
  the way I remember a poem
    memorized when I was a child
      though long forgotten.

I am remembering the words of Her.

I am remembering the word Wisdom
  that She was in the beginning.

I am remembering the Word that

She is.

Like Mother Like Daughter

Because She is beauty
　　I must be beautiful.

Because She is God
　　I must be good.

Because She is everlasting
　　I will continue tomorrow and the day
　　　　after the day after the days after that.

Because She loves me
　　I must be lovable.

And when I pass a mirror
　　when I receive a smile

I recall that way back in the garden
　　or the heaven

I was made in Her image:

Truly in her divine
　　and breathtaking
　　　　image.

Here. In my eyes. Look.

See me.

See Her.

Our Mother in the Movies

Surely you must have noticed in
  Disney movies, along with the catchy songs
    all the dead mothers.

Mother of Ariel—killed by pirates
Mother of Bambi—shot by hunter
Mother of Belle—died from plague
Mother of Nemo—eaten by barracuda
Mother of Tarzan—killed by leopard
Mother of Quasimodo—killed protecting her son
Mother of Cinderella—dead
Mother of Pocahontas—dead
Mother of Snow White—dead

Suspicious, don't you think—such a
  stunningly high rate of maternal mortality
    in one subdivision?

It cries out for an investigation
  which is why I did one
    and here are my findings.

We are the guilty party, you and I
  and our ancestors way back before a camera
    was even a flash in someone's dream.

The storyteller of the tribe is a medicine man
   to our psyches and knows our substrata terrors
      and our needs and draws them into words

and sometimes, if we are lucky, brings remedies
   as in this case, the Tale of the Missing Mother
      and the Miserable Patriarchal Family.

Here we are in the dark, popcorn in hand, gathered
   before the large and flickering fire we call a screen
      ready for a brilliant show and tell.

Actually two stories to tell today, the better to demonstrate
   my dear, this pandemic malady of ours, on a split-screen
      which you can do because this is the movies
         and which I can do because this is a poem.

Shhhhh. Act One: The Motherless House.

Screen One: Captain Von Trapp, military man of Austria
   keeps order with whistle (mother dead, seven children
      good little soldiers, sad, sad, sad).

Screen Two: Mister Banks, agent of Fidelity Fiduciary
   lord of his castle (mother out marching for votes for women
      two children, Jane and Michael, sad, sad, sad).

What can help but heaven? And heaven opens!

Down from the hills comes the aproned woman of song
   with the holy name of Maria, sent by God
      and the Mother Abbess to set the family right.

And simultaneously—

Down from the London sky by umbrella
   comes the woman of magic
      with the holy name of Mary, sent by God
         and the east wind to set the family right.

(I know! For a minute there I was believing that
   Julie Andrews was actually our Heavenly Mother!
      But no, just one of her beautiful daughters
         who got two fabulous roles.)

Act Two: The Woman Turns Things Upside Down.

The Von Trapp children climb trees
   verily the Tree of Life, and warmth
      and music return to the home
         and a smile to the lips of the Captain.

How do you solve a problem like the Goddess?
   You marry her in a grand cathedral blessed by nuns
      and bring healing to the family mortal and divine

and she fortifies the Captain in his courage to
  say no to the fatherland, no to the motherless house
    of the ultra-patriarchal brownshirt Nazis.

And simultaneously—

Poppins unleashes her magic, a lullaby
  a spoonful of sugar and a trip to make-believe
    where we levitate and love to laugh

and step in time with chimney sweeps and see
  that Mary is indeed practically perfect
    every day and in every way

 and we want to feed the birds with our tuppence
    rather than invest in Incorporations! Amalgamations!
      of the highly patriarchal Fidelity Fiduciary Bank.

Act Three: The Healed Family Rises.

And now in this dark theater we celebrate
  as we see our way, feel our way with
    the family Von Trapp stumbling and rising
      climbing, climbing the high green mountain

—up, up, closer, ever closer to heaven.

And look!—the Banks family flying the kite repaired
by father's own hands and trailing mother's
"Votes for Women" banner, useless now
except as a tail to stabilize the kite as it rises

—up, up, into the blue and white sky.

And our communal psyche, stirred by the storyteller
of the tribe, whispers to the full theater, *Yes, yes,*
something holy just happened here.

Wholeness and holiness happened here.

Prayer for Wisdom

Mother God
  I would be a godly mother.

Lady Wisdom
  I would be wise.

I need the wisdom you gave to Solomon
  when he gave the baby to the woman
    who would keep him whole
      rather than keep him hers.

My child is holy.
  I would keep him whole
    even when I am hurt.

Let me not diminish him.

Take my sword
  take all my knives
    the sharp tongue, the cutting glance.

Mother God, Lady Wisdom
  you were there in the beginning
    as Sophia, fashioner of all things
      sharing Heaven's Throne.

I would speak your words
   I would build and not break.

Mother God, Lady Wisdom
   make me wise.

Asking Father

I tiptoed into prayer.

Hesitantly:

"Father, do you mind that I am
   giving so much attention
      to Her these days?"

There were no words.

There was thought.

I thought there was an instant embrace
   warm, I thought, and soft and strong

that drew me in so close
   and drew the Mother in so close

and there we were
   held tight in a circle of three
      a familial trinity.

That's what I thought.

What I know is this:

tears on my cheeks.

Amen.

The Lost Is Found

(Luke, chapter fifteen)

When you enter the parables
  of the three lost things
    you are asked to look past

the cast of earthy characters and see
  in the story that Jesus built

the Divine Family
  three faces of God
    our Father, our Mother, our Brother.

Each character mourns for a missing one:
  the father for the prodigal son
    the woman for the silver coin
      the shepherd for the wayward sheep

each of them a symbol of God who is
  searching for God's beloved child.

Could you tell the story of the prodigal son?
  Certainly.

Could you tell the story of the lost sheep?
  Of course.

Could you tell the story of the lost coin?
  Hmm . . . remind me.

There was a woman who lost a silver coin
  and she lit a candle and swept the house
    diligently, every corner, every crack

and when she found it she called
  her friends and neighbors saying

"Rejoice with me, for I have found
  the piece which was lost!"

Ah, but the story behind the story
  the tale that Jesus was truly telling
    is this:

God the Mother has a precious one
  a silver one, and I have gone astray
    and I am lost

but She will not rest and
  She lights a candle and sweeps the house
    diligently, every corner, every crack

and when She finds me She cries out with joy
  and holds me tight in Her safe hand
    and sings out to the stars:

Rejoice with me, for I have found
  the piece which was lost!

The best stories have layers
  and there is indeed a twist in this tale.

Not only has the story of the coin
  become lost between the cracks
    lost between the prodigal and the sheep

but the woman herself, the Heavenly Woman
  has, in our mortal clumsiness, been misplaced
    somewhere between the Father and the Son.

The tables now are turned
  and I am the one who has lost
    the Coin of Coins, lost my silver Mother
      as She had lost her silver child.

Careless? Stolen? Who can say?
  But I am left bereft and impoverished
    and my children go without.

I have lit my candle.

Long into the night
  I have swept the floors of history

searched the stories of heaven for
   the missing Coin, my missing Mother.

I have diligently probed every corner, every crack
   every space in mind and heart

then suddenly

there She is, shining and rich and round!

I call you now, my neighbors, my friends.

With tears of joy I summon you
   to the long-awaited celebration
      and say to you:

"Rejoice with me for what was lost is found!"

and with the silver of our Mother
   let us purchase a happy ending to the parable:

Wholeness and Peace.

Running Cloud Speaks

In the beginning was Thinking Woman
  who has always existed.

Thinking Woman sends thoughts outward into space
  and whatever She thinks comes into being.

She thought the rocks and the clouds
  and the snow and the juniper trees
    and the clear rivers and they appeared.

She thought the rabbit and the deer
  and the fish and the wolf and the buffalo
    and they walked on the earth or swam in the river.

She thought the turquoise and the shells
  and the silver and all that is beautiful
    and it happened as She thought it would.

She thought the medicine for healing.

She thought me.

She thought you.

She thought all the children
  and all the women and all the men
    who think of Her in return and in gratitude.

She thought the words
  that I am speaking to you now.

A Goddess of the East

Long before the troubles
  that we observe in Islam there was peace
    and there were poems and songs and odes
      to the Divine Mother.

I read that Muhammad said
  "Paradise is at the feet of the Mother"
    and shame on me for my surprise.

Everywhere in history the longer and farther
  you look the larger looms the image
    of the Heavenly Woman.

Everywhere She was perceived
  everywhere She was lost
    everywhere She emerges again

like a moon moving the ocean
  like a messenger whispering a word
    in the wind and the word is "rise."

I have watched the rise of a young goddess of the East
  Malala by name, who took a bullet to the head
    for her hunger to sit at a desk.

Divinity can drop from heaven like rain or angels
   or it can rise from earth like green undaunted grass

or like girls carrying books
   fierce girls who are prepared to die
      for words.

Two Sides of One Precious Coin

His Holiness the Dalai Lama
　　he who is a smiling sun, said:

"The world will be saved
　　by the Western woman."

Yin has been so patient.

From Buddhism came Taoism
　　and the famous circle halved with a curve
　　　　that looks to me like two lovely

tear drops comforting one another
　　with a small round heart
　　　　of the other inside each.

Feminine the yin
　　the dark, the shady side of the hill.

Masculine the yang
　　the bright, the sunny side of the hill.

Yin the negative
　　the passive female principle.

Yang the positive
　　the active male principle.

China anciently judged the value of the two
   as we might judge coins: one bronze, one gold

all of which created the Chinese patriarchy

which gifted girls with strips of cloth
   to pinch life from their feet

and gifted girl babies
   with a cradle of rushing river

and gifted the heavens and the earth
   with the extermination of the Asian sun goddess
      whose names are many.

Yin is running out of patience.
   I believe I heard her whisper that

she is weary of centuries of captivity
   in that limited round that has crushed
      too many like an emperor's wheel.

Yin and the Goddess of Heaven
   who are kin are calling
      the women of the West

to step to the front because
   we have tools like universities
      and money and democracy

and because we are a fearless
    and gentle warrior
        with sword and heart and hearth.

As goddess Tara, the Divine Woman
    asks His Holiness to speak.

As God the Mother, the Divine Woman
    asks me to speak.

As the Awakened Feminine, She asks
    women who are without tradition to speak.

And the men.

Yin speaks to Yang and tells him
    the times they are a-changing
        and in all her names the Divine Woman
            speaks to the men of the West.

She asks them to speak too for they are rapidly
    learning to value the woman not as bronze
        learning that her passive has become active
            learning that the world can be saved only

by the female and the male purchasing salvation
    together, two sides of one precious gold coin.

The Chinese "Book of Documents" says that
  when the hen announces the dawn
    it signals the arrival of terrible things
      and perhaps even the sky will fall.

This morning I stand on the step and happily sing:
  "The day dawn is breaking
    the world is awaking . . . ."

Indeed it will be a beautiful day.

Holy the Marriage Bed

The ancient Kabbalah of the Jews
   issues the happiest commandment of worship

for it tells the story of the banishment
   of the Shekinah, the feminine part of God

who was separated from her Eternal Love
   by the sins of man, which brought a universal disaster
      one we see today through shattered windows

and God mourns the loss as only God can mourn
   and we mourn too but know not for what we mourn

and only when humans come together in love
   can the Holy Shekinah be reunited with Her God
      and female and male glory again as One

and therefore the commandment
   from the ancient Kabbalah that on Shabbat

after the baking of the sacred braided bread
   after the prayer and the lighting of the candles

after midnight a man and his wife
   must be coupled in the marriage bed
      and worship God in the temple of one another

for their coupling assists God and His Shekinah
  to couple and to become One as they should be One

and from their Oneness the Shekinah
  delivers the souls of humans

and from their Oneness the world will be healed.

Behold, thou art fair, my beloved,
  also our bed is green.
    Come, O Bride . . . Come, O Bride.

Phoebe the Shaker

Oh, bless the day Mother Ann Lee found me
   on the auction block and shamed the white man
      that owned me into lettin' me go a free woman!

And she took me in and my first night there
   I cry 'cause I was thinkin' about my three
      children that was sold away from me

and Mother Ann come in and she put her arms
   around me and she ask me if I was sold from
      my mother and I say yes, I was

and she say then I must hold to the breast
   of the Heavenly Mother, who has never
      sold a child and never will

and I say I never heard of such a Mother
   and Mother Ann ask me if I was born of a
      father and a mother and I say of course

and she say that I must look up through nature
   to God, that our natural parents are like the
      Perfect Parents who created us

our Father and Mother which are in heaven!

You ever heard of such a thing?
  Well, I was near struck dumb!

And Mother Ann say, Well, child, do you see
  the human world and the animal world all
    walkin' around lookin' like they was
      formed out of three masculine beings?

And I say, Why, no, everything comes in twos
  don't it, right down to the little field mice
    that are male and female.

And she say, That right, child, and God is the
  Eternal Two and when the Father and the Mother
    are near to us it is the season of love!

Well, I stay awake cryin' it was so beautiful.

And then I slept, and in my sleep I remember
  oh, I remember what my mama sang to me
    and her mama sang to her and all the

Mamas sang back to Africa, about that great
  shinin' black Mother of us all!

And in my sleep I lay in the lap of that
  Great Mother and she stroke my hair
    and she say

Shhhh, honey, it gonna be all right.
  Someday it all gonna be all right 'cause
    you is my baby and I is your Mama forever!

And she sing me a lullaby
  and oh, I slept so good.

Young Female Buddhist Today

My grandmother said to me:

"Women cannot reach enlightenment
 unless they gain good karma
  and are reborn as men.

Observe the doctrine and
 cleanse your karma every day
  my child."

I said to my grandmother:

"The wheel of time keeps turning
 and I have spoken to the Great Mother
  the Womb from which all Buddhas flow

and She told me that right living
 is all that is required and that
  my karma ran over our dogma

and She takes great joy
 in my being a woman
  and so, Grandmother, do I."

Seeing Mary

My next-door neighbor Joan
    after I shared my Motherless poems with her
        said to me:

"How I wish you were a Catholic.
    You could have Mary!"

Mary, Mother of Jesus, Mother of God.
    Mary, hold the broken me
        a thin pietà in your holy arms.

Her people see her, the divine and female
    face they yearn for, they actually *see* her
        and I am amazed.

She comes to them, the mystic, the peasant
    in vision, in brilliant apparition.

I get to see Mary once a year.
    Reverently I loosen the shroud of newspaper
        that has covered her blue-and-white

plaster of Paris self in the box in the garage
    along with the baby and the shepherds
        the entire cast of Christmas

scratched and chipped every one
  and two with heads glued back on
    from ninety years of family adoration.

Adoration!
  That's the key, I think.

Billions have paved a path to Mary's heart
  praying the rosary daily or more
    beckoning her with loving fingers.

And She comes—Our Lady of Guadalupe
  leaving Castilian roses and a miracle image

Our Lady of Fatima leaving warnings
  and signs in the sky

Our Lady of Lourdes leaving healings.

Hundreds more
  and how does it happen?

Maybe the power of the prayers
  the adoration of billions is irresistible
    and creates the path.

Do they simply love her

into sight?

"I Want to Do That!"

We have chased the tale of Eve's
  disobedience for centuries
    and it has gotten us nowhere.

In the poem that is Eve
  here is how it happened:

She saw the tree
  the Tree of Life.

She watched the growing and the greening
  the blossoming and the bursting
    and she said:

"I want to do that!"

And so she took the first sweet bite
  carefully, carefully going about
    her Mother's business.

Sunbeam Story

When I was little and learned that
  Jesus wants me for a sunbeam
    (the narrow shaft of bright that shoots
      through the screen)

I figured something was up
  something strange and wonderful.

And when I learned from the new physics
  that I am formed of light
    formed of star stuff

I was sure of it
  and I shone as a good sunbeam should.

But then I remembered that Christ
  who lights the world said
    that I should do works like unto his

that my own light is not a narrow shaft
  and it's time to throw off that bushel.

I am no longer small.

I see skies that are too dark
  I see nights that are too long
    and I see with wondering awe that

Jesus wants me for a sunrise.

What to Do

When the thing happened
   that slammed my breath shut
     and knocked me to my knees

I cried, "God, what can I do?"

He said: *Wrestle.*
   Wrestle with it until you wrest
     some words from it.

She said: *With the words build a story.*

He said: *Or a poem.*

She said: *Then cease the wrestling*
   and the wresting and just

rest.

I Heard God Singing

Earth the garden—

Time the season—

Soul the harvest—

Love the reason.

The Push and the Pull of Birthing

That tunnel they speak of
   those who know a taste of death
      and come back to tell the bliss
         of the magnetic rushing pull through dark
            toward bright beyond words

is it also a cosmic birth canal, a tunnel
   of two-way traffic?

Is it the largeness of the smallness
   of the passage that the mother of my flesh
      groaned me through, pushed me through

out of her dark womb
   into this sunlit world?

And when the nine months times ninety or more
   of my breathing in and breathing out are done
      according to plan

when I am the one who mothers myself
   through the hard work
      the labor pain of dying

will I then be delivered through the
   death-into-birth canal that pulls me into the
      reaching arms of my original Mother?

She who conceived the thought of me
  and now receives the abundance of me
    planted a while in earth

She who will joyfully watch and tend
  and feed my eternal becoming.

Finding My Roots

I had my ancestry done.

It was quite simple
  as they had promised.

I sent in a few streams of thought
  a smudge of heart
    and it came back just as I'd hoped:

I am one hundred percent godly.

The paternal line was easily traced
  as it's been heavily traveled
    for millennia.

The maternal line not so much.

It's been long ignored
  and even obscured
    but the demand is surging.

One hundred percent godly
  and on both sides!

It wasn't really a surprise.

Just good to know.

Night Ritual of Three Mothers

I sleep tonight under my mother's blanket
  pink-and-white checkered and wool.

Last year a brother sent out a photo asking
  "Does anyone remember this blanket?
    Does anyone want this blanket?"

I was the only one who said, "Yes and yes!"

At first glimpse I remembered the pattern
  the scent, the wooliness, the motherness.

It may have been a gift or a treasured
  purchase from the Utah Woolen Mills
    from quarters and dimes saved.

Something beautiful and warm
  not like the newspapers she used to layer
    between blankets to protect her five children
      from the winters of the Uintah Basin.

Her name was Emeline.
  She died when I was fifteen.

It is soon winter and three-blanket weather.
   I arrange her blanket nearest, just above the sheet
      and I climb into bed and smooth
         a place for my mother to sit.

She is here and she puts a hand on my head
   and sings the words she sang before
      words I too have sung:

"Baby's boat's a silver moon . . ."

Then I reach to lift the covers and draw her
   into bed with me and we are sisters now
      and we whisper like

the girls in a Jane Austen novel
   and the pink-and-white checkered
      wool blanket warms us both.

Then I reach again way beyond
   the baby's boat and the silver moon
      back generations and millennia and eons

and I invite our First Mother to join us.

Sometimes I call her Ema.
   She never dies.

She spun the threads that we are
  and She wove us well.
    We are tighter than wool
      and beautiful in design.

She fills the room and is willing to be seen
  if we close our eyes.

She is brilliant as stained glass with the sun behind.
  Her crown is of stars and music is on Her lips
    as our Holy Comforter asks if we are
      ready for our lullaby.

Then She pulls the blanket a little closer
  and we are three mothers
    two beneath and One above

and with a hand on each heart
  She sings us to sleep.

Heavenly Mother's Lullaby

I close all the curtains, I turn out the light,
I tuck the night around you.
Your toys are away now, the day's in its drawer.
My arms once more have found you.

Sleep, sleep, sleep will bring you home.
Once a day, from far away
I gently bring you home,
I gently bring you home.

We'll stop and remember why you went away,
Why you won't stay forever.
We'll smile at your good times, we may dry some tears.
We'll plan the years together.

Sleep, sleep, sleep will bring you home.
Once a day, from far away
I gently bring you home,
I gently bring you home.

You will not recall it, you'll wake with the dawn.
Your life goes on in daylight.
But there may be something, the drift of a dream,
A thought that seems to stay bright.

Sleep, sleep, sleep will bring you home.
Once a day, from far away
I gently bring you home,
I gently bring you home.

Before Prayer

Wondering tonight if I really do love God
  or if I just love the idea of God.

Maybe God actually is an idea.

A smart physicist said that the universe
  begins to look more like a thought
    than a thing.

A thought is an idea
  so the thought that God is an idea
    interests me.

Is God the First Thought?
  The First Thinker?
    I think . . . therefore I am the Great I Am.

The God I was given
  is not always a good idea
    for there are reports of vengeance.

And tonight I am thinking
  (for I believe I am a thought of God
    and therefore I think)

that the true God
  is the most superb idea that ever was
    an idea that became Creator.

Once God whispered: *I Am Love.*

There is no more excellent thought than Love
   so a God who is Love is the ideal idea.

Words are the confetti of thoughts.

I try to catch the divine ones high
   scoop them as they fall
     pick them out of the carpet
       press them into an inadequate poem

and even though the Thought
  is no longer whole
    the pieces still are holy

and I am quite certain tonight
  that I love my idea of God.

Growing up Godly

I was a child of God
  and then my DNA moved me to become
    a grown-up of God.

My ancestors had children so they could grow up
  to help with the mowing and the haying
    and the sewing and the baking.

What does God need children for?
  He is not a farmer
    She does not run a kitchen.

God, being the Great Thought, needs
  I believe, help with the thinking
    for creation is vast and will never be filled.

Bad men have said, "You and the land
  belong to me:
    my thought is your command."

Good men have said,
  "Just listen to me for that is the
    order of things."

Silly men have said, "Don't you worry
  your pretty little head about that.
    Don't worry about it!"

God spoke to me this morning and said:

How I love the thought of you.
  Here's another day—
    just think what you can do.

What Good Is God?

God the noun.
  Good the adjective.
    A simple "o" varies them.

Last night exhausted not from the day
  but from the burdens, the perennial
    grief, the confusion

all of which I knew would
  wake me in the morning
    with a cold kiss

I mouthed not a prayer but a question:

"What good is God?
  Truly. What good is God?"

I listened, hoping I might hear
  some goodly explanation.

Crickets.

I had discovered that God
  is not a good conversationalist
    so I made up this exchange:

"Dear God, is watching the world
  just spectator sport to you?
    Couldn't you get a little more involved?

All these prayers, God . . . what's the use?"

*So you think you have prayed for bread
  and I've given you a stone?*

"You could put it that way."

*Even if that were true, which it is not
  what would your friend Jesus
    tell you to do about it?*

"Do? Like . . . ?"

*Like return good for evil . . . love your enemies . . .
  bless those that curse you . . .*

"I didn't say you cursed me."

*Like pray for those that mistreat you
  or give you a stone instead of bread.*

"Pray for you?" I laughed.
  "Pray for God?"

If I don't answer your prayers
  you could answer mine
    that's what Jesus would say.

"You pray?"

Without ceasing.

"For what?"

I pray that you will not give me a stone
  but that you will give me bread
    that you will feed my sheep

feed my sheep.

I kept waking in the night as warm little kisses
  reminded me of the time after time dear ones
    had lifted my stones
      had given me bread

had fed this little sheep.

Chiasm on the Being of God

There is no God.

    So.

      Here.

        I will have to lean in and do

         just a tiny bit

        of what God should do.

      There.

    Oh.

There is God.

What If?

In spite of our stories
  of betrayal and sadness

what if you and I

and every child pushed crying
  into this world have safely traveled
    the meadow's meandering paths

hand in hand with the Mother on one side
  and the Father on the other

who walk with us and then run and on 1-2-3
  lift us high, scared and squealing
    and then let gravity bring us down laughing
      or sometimes weeping

their hands still tight around ours.

Our Mother and Her Dove

I sent out a dove to find the Mother
  and I left the window open.

The Mother whose signature was the dove
  in ancient days, written with a flourish
    of feathers, white against blue.

So many of the first goddesses
  were known by the doves in their hands
    or the doves in their hair.

There was Asherah of the groves
  the Tree of Life sprung from Mother Earth
    and adopted as the Hebrew Goddess.

The wind came, the wind lifting the dove
  and shaking the tree, the *ruach*, the wind
    the breath, the spirit, a force all feminine.

The Spirit of God, *Ruach Elohim,* was
  hovering over the waters and Her children
    knew She was the female presence

the indispensable aspect of the God that
  created them in God's own image
    created them male and female.

She suckled the Hebrews
    and fed the early Christians
        and they gave thanks to her as Mother

their Mother whom they called the Holy Spirit
    whose dove descended to bless
        the baptism of Jesus

that same dove I sent out
    when I left the window open.

History has drawn an unholy curtain
    between us and our ancient Mother
        but I pulled back the veil and I saw.

Here's what they did, the monks who
    translated to please the powers that be
        and the powers were he.

At the stroke of a quill the Hebrew "she"
    became the Greek "it" and then the English "he"
        and no one cared as the bright

feminine words fluttered to the cold floor
    like clipped wings of a dove.

But can a Mother forget her child?
    Or a child forget her Mother?

I sent out a dove to find Her
　　and I left the window open.

The dove is sister to the homing pigeon
　　so I knew she could find her way back.

I had touched her sweet soft head
　　and she knew the scent of me.

I sent out a dove and she returned.

She fluttered through the window
　　to my open hand.

A note was tied to her leg
　　a little scroll written by the One
　　　　for whom she is a sign.

It read:

Dear One,

Please forgive the monks.

I know you love poetry
so here are three haiku
from me to you:

The past is dust and
dissolves in one small gust of
God's eternity.

Feel the wind shifting.
Feel the Ruach Elohim
Sweep across the land.

Feel me move through the
Holy of Holies of your
heart and build a nest.

Love to all.
Please tell the others.

I write back to Her each evening
  in my prayers.

Sometimes I call her Holy Spirit.

Often merely

Mother.

Under Your Wings

Divine Mother

Gather me as promised
  gather me as a hen gathers
    her chicks under her wings.

Sweep me to you now with feathers
  soft and strong.

A storm comes and the violent sky
  cracks loud and open.

The rain would wash me
  like a leaf into the stream.

Press the fragile fearful ball of me
  close to your dear body
    warm and remembered.

Safe silence is under
  the quick beat of your heart.

Divine Mother
  leave me not to the storm.

Gather me
  gather me
    gather me

under your beautiful as angel
  wings.

Two of Every Kind

In that story about Noah and the ark
  is it even possible that the God who was
    disappointed unto destruction

in the people He had created
  but amended His condemnation to allow
    the survival of two of every kind

male and female

so that those creatures
  could create more creatures
    because creation requires

both male and female
  and therefore is it even possible that

He the Creator of all creation

could be the only One
  in heaven or on earth that does not
    come two of every kind?

Look at Them:
  the magnificent He and the stupendous She
    the Two that are One
      and the One that is Two

speaking to the always disappointing
  and always loved children
    not words of condemnation but salvation

watching all of us floating along
  in our fear of water
    and our fear of God

while God lures us to dry land as
  He sends olive leaf after olive leaf and
    She sends dove after dove.

Saving Mother Earth

What if our planet's illness
  is partly a problem of gender?

What if its birth announcement
  when creation settled
    had not been "It's a girl!"

which in earliest times was the highest
  compliment, for earth and woman
    were twin bringers of life

and it wasn't until the undoing that
  the phrase became "Only a girl!"
    and the boys decided that

bigger was better and strongest was best
  and raised *him* above *her* on the
    pronoun totem pole and soon

the word *conquer* comes to mind followed by
  the words *chattel* and *rape*, after which
    the female and the female earth were never safe.

I have to wonder—

What if in the beginning the males had seen
    the earth as just one of the boys or better yet
        as the Boss whom they had to please?—

the Chief, the Master who paid their wages in deer
    and water and minerals and mushrooms
        and demanded excellent care.

But that ship has sailed and so my best hope
    is this:

What if today, because the gender climate
    has changed and women put men in prison
        for what used to be mere male privilege

 what if the rising respect for the female
    in all her offices from birthing a baby
        to leading a nation

what if that powerful respect continues to rise
    rise higher and higher like healing waters
        until it trickles down

trickles down

to cover the injured body of

our Mother the Earth.

Turning Things Upside Down to Help the Men and Boys Understand

The father and his boy have counted the days
   and here they are up at the lake
      that mirrors the moon

with a gathering of others on a fathers and sons
   weekend and the day has been
      glorious and sunny and sweaty.

Tents have been raised and sleeping bags laid
   and Orion found and fish caught
      and cleaned and fried and finished
         along with the pork and beans.

Now the campfire's crackle begins to die
   and there's no more s'mores
      and even if this were all, this one night

it would have been so worth the planning
   and the packing and the overtime
      for this father to be here

here with his arm around his nine-year-old boy
   who leans into him with trust
      and shines with more than campfire in his eyes.

And they sing just one more song
   that great spiritual that still rocks
      that comfort song that feels like a happy prayer:

She's got the whole world in Her hands
She's got the whole world in Her hands
She's got the whole world in Her hands
She's got the whole world in Her hands

and the other verses led by the shouts of
   those who can remember that

She's got you and me, sister, in Her hands
She's got you and me, brother, in Her hands . . .

. . .and the little bitty baby . . .

. . .and the sun and the rain . . .

. . .and the wind and the clouds . . .

. . .and the ocean and the seas . . .

. . .and the moon and the stars . . .

She's got everybody here and everybody there
She's got the whole world in Her hands.

Smiling, the father and his boy
   retire to their tent

and gaze out the mesh window at the
moon and the stars, the very ones
that She holds safely in Her hands.

It Shall Be Given

Learning that God is not
   a handyman
I have ceased to ask Him
   to fix things.

Learning that God is not
   a handmaid
I no longer expect Her
   to bring stuff and keep me safe.

Happy now to know that God
   is the great abundant Thought
      we commune.

I speak fear
   and I read my name written
      on the palm of a godly hand.

I speak lost
   and I feel a map carved like braille
      upon my heart.

I speak despair
   and I watch a flower blossom
      after snow
         yellow by yellow by yellow.

I speak need
   and I see a light in my mind
      sufficient for one step.

I speak thank you
   and I sense a smile.

Question and Answer with Jesus

Me:
About that mountain, Jesus
   no one's faith has ever moved it, you know
      and there's some guilt around that.

Jesus:
Dear friend, for a poet you seem
   slow at spotting metaphor.
      I was a poet too, you know.

I like what I did with
   the mustard seed.

Hear me.

Close your eyes and see the mountain
   in your mind, the big unbudging, mindless
      mountain that really needs moving.

Send three white doves to lift it
   by its peaks, lift it like a leaf
      and give it to the wind.

Mountains can hide things.
   Behold! The golden sun rises on a blue sea
      and you would never have known.

But a greater miracle still.
  Let the sun's rays find you
    and fill you and overflow you.

Now, dear friend, not only can you be a poet
  you can be a poem!—
    one that I wrote:

You can be the light of the world.

Jesus Remembered

I am imagining this morning
   after my amen in his name

that when our Mother helped Jesus
   prepare for his thirty-three-year
      mission into the world's wilderness

She laid a hand on his heart and said:

Don't forget this:

Of the many people you will teach
   and bless and heal, pay special attention
      to the ones who look like me.

Things have gone awry, as we knew
   they might and many are badly used

especially your sisters who are seen as
   property and positioned five feet lower
      in the temple than the men

and are kept from the scriptures
   and from speaking
      and are subordinate everywhere

and oh the daily prayers your Father hears
   from our dear Jewish boys:

"Praised be God that he has not
   created me a woman."

You will not forget your Mother's words.
   You will pay special attention
      to the ones who look like me.

I am imagining that She watched carefully
   as he walked the dusty earth doing shocking things
      that made their way into my Bible

and perhaps into his Mother's journal:

He spoke today to a woman in public—
   a Samaritan!—at Jacob's well—
      disreputable act, they say.

He calls women from their houses to come and listen
   and follow him as disciples, ministering to him.
      Unheard of, they say.

Today he allowed a woman (of ill repute they say)
   to wash his feet with her tears
      and dry them with her hair. I wept.

He performs miracle after miracle at the request
   of those who look like me.

He saved a woman from stoning by calling out
  our dear hypocritical boys
    the scribes and Pharisees.

Ah, to sweet Martha and Mary
  he speaks of the life of the spirit and the mind
    as "the better part" of the busyness of women.

He calls women to pray, to lead
  to preach the gospel—such good news!

He remembered!

Sitting here now with the thin pages that
  softly rustle as I turn them, I feel Jesus
    laying a hand on my heart and saying to me:

Do what ye have seen me do.

And I believe he asks me to pay special attention
  to those who look like our Mother.

I remember.

Easter

Wondering now what Jesus would say
  about the day on which we
    celebrate his rising

bearing the name of an ancient heathen goddess
  of spring, Eostre, whom you find in the folds
    of the old religion of the Anglo-Saxons

a people so devoted to the goddess who
  annually breathed new life into the world
    she with her eggs and hares and hot-cross buns

that the conquering Christians sent from Rome
  allowed the people to keep her name on this
    auspicious day and grafted into

Eostre's Tree of Life a new branch
  one that honored the resurrection
    of the Lord Jesus Christ.

Wondering now how Jesus would feel
  about the inherited name and the pagan
    overlay on the holy day of his rising

always to be celebrated on the first Sunday
   after the full moon occurring on or after
      the vernal equinox.

The Jesus that I know would
   I believe, smile and say

My friends, we rise together.

Christ's Garden

I am told that he was
   the firstborn of our Mother Father
      fashioned exquisitely in the fresh heart of heaven.

Was our Mother midwife to his mortal birth
   gently funneling his fullness
      into the tiny body in the manger

and singing praises with the angels
   singing glory and peace and goodwill to all?
      —for these things She had taught her son.

Did She celebrate the holy act
   of his baptism with the gift of a dove
      bringing a white breath of heaven?

And was She the One storied by Luke
   who came to him in the garden
      on the night of agony?

Did She hold him, wrap him in
   his Mother's love
      bathe his face with Her tears

strengthening him
  strengthening him

a hand on his head and a hand on his heart
  reminding him of the power planted
    in him before the world was

power to bear not only the pain of the cross
  but the pain of the evil of the fallen world
    that cut deeper than thorns or nails
      and would soon burst his hero's heart

strengthening him
  strengthening him.

Did She sing to him through the night
  sing until his hour came
    until the cock crowed?

My Garden

I am not exceptional
    like my elder brother
        in Gethsemane.

My garden a small untidy room
    my suffering stone size and barely
        the weight to break a heart

but barely broken is enough.

Too slight am I to request a vigil
    even an embrace, though just a touch
        across my cheek would be enough

enough to strengthen me.

Psalm

Mother, speak the words again.

In the beginning there was darkness
  upon the face of the deep and the Elohim
    moved upon the darkness and spoke

and their words were:

Let there be light

and there was light.

This day there is darkness
  upon the dead sea of my soul.
    I stumble and cannot rise.

The sun freezes before it hits
  my heart, my harp.
    I cannot pluck and I cannot sing.

I am a child who calls for my Mother.

Deliver me now from darkness.
  Speak again the words you spoke
    in the beginning:

Let there be light.

I will speak the words after you, Mother.
  I will speak them with you.
    We will speak them together until it is so.

Let there be light
  Let there be light
    Let there be light.

Don's Daughter

I celebrate the birth of this girl child
  with the joy of an ancient Hebrew
    celebrating the birth of a boy.

With bells or trumpets or cards or calls
  her birth is worth celebrating.

See how her mother smiles
  (though that is no surprise).

But, oh, see how her father kneels
  at the cradle of this little goddess
    with worship in his eyes.

In Celebration of the First Menstruation

Katy, who had of late been putting
   pads and panties on her Keeshond dog
      Briget Baby Brown Eyes

loped long-legged and twelve and sweet
   into my room and giggled
      "Mom, Mom, I'm in heat! I just started!"

I pulled her down into the big chair
   that we used to not quite fill
      and made sure she understood

that a menstruating woman
   is of the devil, that she must not
      look at the sun, sit in water

speak to a man for she is unclean
   or enter a church
      for she would defile it.

And I stroked her innocent freckled
   skin and bright braided hair
      and told her to keep in mind

that she is as St. Jerome said
   formed of foul slime.

Katy laughed. "Right, Mom!"

And I told her all that was from
    a bad period, men's period
        when male was god and jealous

a period that luckily
        menopaused.

But that there was an earlier time
    when women's secret was sacred
        when the Great Goddess

gave the blood of life
    and all worshipped joyously
        at her royal fountain

when girls "bore the flower"
    a flower that flows a future fruit
        making her a marvel

a time that is due again.

Then I gave Katy five and said
    "Hey, woman, let's go celebrate!"

And we went right out under the sun
    and Katy spoke right up to the man
        and ordered a BLT and we ate.

We clicked our cups to flowering
  and Katy giggled and blushed and bounced
    and blessed the restaurant

with her holy presence.

The Voice of God

I asked my friend
  "So how do you know that God is male?"

He laughed. "Didn't you see
  The Ten Commandments?
    Didn't you hear the Voice of God?"

"Well," I said, "that was only because
  Katharine Hepburn was not available."

Actually I met the Voice of God in person.

His name was Delos Jewkes and years ago
  both of our voices were requested at an event
    where he sang and I recited a poem

and oh, indeed, the Voice of God
  was cavernous as Carlsbad

and standing before him you had an impulse
  to hang on to something.

But would it not have been lovely if Cecil B. DeMille
  had offered us a godly duet of Jewkes and Hepburn
    pronouncing in sync from a stereophonic heaven?

For in the beginning They were One
　　our singular and plural Elohim
　　　in whose image we were made
　　　　male and female.

And when They spoke
　　the exquisite vibration of their Word

created all.

The Name

"God Is Not a Boy's Name"
  is a thought more huge
    than a T-shirt can hold.

 God is not embarrassed
   to wear the pink of sunset or to
     dress in the flowered print of hills.

God does not prefer the truck
  to the baby doll.

God has never created a boy's club
   and put a sign up
     that puts girls down.

God showers a blessing on each conception
  showers with indiscriminate love.

He blesses the Y chromosome.

She blesses the X chromosome.

The results are equally divine
  and equally fine
    though blessedly not quite the same.

And sadly, stumbling through
   the maze of mortality
      they often equally forget that

God is not a boy's name.

Crime Against the Flying Ones

Whoever it was at the corporate table
  that performed the crime
    against the tribes of the flying ones

reaching with his long arm and pushing
  Mother Nature aside to steal from their nests
    the words "twitter" and "tweet"

owes the birds and God an apology.

The guilty one should serve time, time spent
  lying on the green grass observing the
    soaring and coasting of robins and wrens

the former proprietors of twitters and tweets

and he should listen as they voice uncounted syllables
  joyful exclamations across the trees
    of who knows what
      maybe a worm, maybe a sunset.

We are less moral than the birds.

The seagull that left a white and innocent turd
  on your windshield or your hair
    would surely tweet if he could
      "Sorry, nothing personal."

But we toss tweet after tweet of deliberate crap
   across the airwaves and pass it on and on
      and rub it in and seldom apologize

for our words are apart from our faces
   something no respectable bird
      who stands by her sound would ever do:

Blackbird still speaks like the first bird.

They are not the poorer, but we are
   for our vocabulary has been violated
      and our most serious words now sound
         like a laughing matter.

To hear on the news:

"The President of the United States just tweeted that
a deadly military strike has occurred . . ."

I picture him sitting on a branch and smiling
   with music notes around his head.

The bird world deserves an apology for the theft.

God does too, God who was the first Word
   God who beautifully spoke the world into being

and whose eye is on the sparrow.

Position

If "A" looks up to "B"
   then by nature of the physical universe
      "B" must look down on "A"

rather like two birds
   positioned one on a tree
      and one on the ground.

Or so thought Marjorie
   who had always wanted to marry
      a man she could look up to

but wondered where that would
   place *her* if she did.

Imagine her astonishment when she
   met Michael and found that together
      they stood physics on its head.

You could never draw this on paper
   for it defies design

but year after year they lived
   a strange arrangement that by
      all known laws could not occur:

She looked up to him

and he looked up to her.

To the Wave of Women We Have Sent to Washington

Realizing that an estrogen-free zone
   can be a dangerous place
      we know your gender will be a bonus.

So don't forget the hearth.

Pack the sword for it may come to that
   and there may be a mountain
      you are willing to die on.

But don't forget the hearth.

It is already packed deep in your DNA
   a gift from millennia where women
      sparked the fire and nourished
         the tribe and taught the children

we do not hurt one another.

Inside the hearth is the heart
   without which nothing can survive.

You are the hearth keeper.

Throw out every useless thing.

But keep the hearth.

Woman Creating

That woman you want to
  evict from the hall because
    she wishes to nurse her baby—

People should pay to see her.

She should be placed on a cushioned oak rocker
  on a round riser with soft lighting
    and encircled with protective tape
      yellow tape with bold black letters:

AWE ALERT—SCENE OF A MIRACLE IN PROGRESS

And nearby should be a framed sign
  with words in skilled calligraphy:

> *This woman recently created and birthed the body*
> *of a small human with over fifteen trillion cells*
> *three hundred bones, ten thousand taste buds*
> *a brain with ten million nerve cells*
> *and a heart that beats*
> *one hundred and thirty times a minute.*
>
> *At this moment she is gifting the child*
> *with an elixir that could not be duplicated*
> *in the laboratory of a Nobel Prize–winning scientist*
> *a recipe that has been developing over*

millions of years of female creativity
and the first food on the face of the earth
clearly given God's stamp of approval.

Your reverence is appreciated.

Matriarchal Blessing

I have blessed you, you know.

Not hands on head but body around body
   nine months encircled
     by the liquid sound of my light

uttering not promises
   but miracles cell by cell

giving not admonitions
   but affirmations of
     your natural splendor.

You receive and you are my blessing
   a blessing that I author
     by the power of the holy

that I bear and that I share
   by love ordained

and through which I pronounce you
   blessed forever.

Observe!

A woman who knows heaven
  better than I do said to me:
    God does not come *to* you
      God comes *through* you.

Maybe it's like that odd business
  of the dual nature of light in which
    it functions as a particle or a wave

and which of the two shows up
  depends on the observer.

Perhaps in the beginning
  the God of Light was a wave

and She observed and moved
  and there came particles of water
    and He observed and moved
      and there came particles of land.

Maybe I, a being of light, sit like a particle
  still as a breathing bump on a log
    and then God exclaims:

Observe!

And when I hear God say: *Observe!*
  I notice, and I, the little particle, become a wave
    as God comes not to me but through me

and we move.

We are a wave that moves upon the sick and the sad
  and the poor and the abused and the castaway
    and we move upon a blank piece of paper.

With practice I sit on the log
  and speak to myself
    my particle self and say: *Observe!*

And I hear and I see, and wavelike I move
  for I have learned the movements of God
    who comes through me

the movements of creation
  the movements of healing
    the movements of joy.

Of Angels and Men

Angels in the Bible always manifest
  masculine, never "she," never "it"
    always a transcendent "he" and often a warrior.

But then came the artists and from Rembrandt
  to Hallmark we see legions of lady angels
    lovely and smiling and often with wings.

Which makes me think that maybe
  like beauty
    or a Rorschach test—

heaven is in the eye of the beholder.

The Omni Factor

Needing your presence tonight, Mother
   I invite you.

Then I think of the woman on the
   other side of the planet whose child
     has ribs like a washboard

and eyes dark and empty and huge
   and I say, "No, she needs you
     more than I do."

But then I remember the happy mystery:

You are the Woman of the Omnis
   omnipresent and available
     to all who say, "Please come."

Of your several omnis this one
   is my personal favorite
     top of the list of godly powers.

Science may explain some day
   as the search continues for the arrow of time
     qubit entanglement, quantum gravity and such

explain just how the fine, fine matter of God
   can sift swifter than light and show up
      to fill the smallest request

so that He is present here
   and She is present now
      omni and always.

When child became children for me
   I was split and exhausted having to
      choose between here and there.

You have no here and there
   and never have to prioritize
      your billions, Mother.

That's the awesomeness of godness.

So I will take my full portion now, not part
   but the whole of your holy presence as we sit
      together by the fire in my specific home

and admire the melody of rain on window
   and watch my secrets dance between us:
      my sweetness, my silliness.

You observe me with unveiled adoration
   as if this moment and this place
      is the only thing imaginable.

And I accept your generous care knowing that
    my omnipresent Mother is also on the other
        side of the planet in a little hut

holding another daughter through the
    unavoidable grief of this mortal world.

Love Poem

I was trying to fall asleep last night
   but I fell into poetry

and who was I to ignore
   all those friendly words
     waving at me?

Hours passed with me immersed
   in delicious new thought
     and now and then

without opening an eye

reaching to the other pillow where my
   notebook sleeps and is always at the ready
     to receive my scribbles.

I woke up really tired but still smiling
   and willing to pay the price this morning
     for a night of love.

Imagine

And if it turns out
  dear Mother Father God
    that you were just my

Imaginary Friend

(though I would never know
  would I?—for then death is a dark room
    getting smaller).

Still I will thank your make-believe
  Self for delivering actual warmth
    and actual light.

And then the question must arise:
  what is the source of that
    manifestly friendly and divine

Imagination of Mine?

Grace

That glistening reservoir of God's grace—
   is it available for the tiny things
      or is it reserved for big violations

like the ones we read about in the papers
   that require a full bath of body and soul?

I don't expect ever to need a radical cleanse
   have blood on my hands
      or only hate where heart should be

so may I just take sips when I'm ungracious
   may I dip my small cup into the fullness
      and drink until I am filled with grace?

Filled
   until next time.

The First Love Story

I know God is Love
  but is God *in* love?

Is God totally crazy about each other?

The vaults of history hold hundreds of myths
  telling how the world came to be:
    that it was birthed from the

golden womb of a goddess, or that a powerful
  sword-wielding warrior god fashioned
    it from a goddess's body.

And who dares to think they own the one true tale
  even today when we have telescopes and
    popes and prophets that can spy on heaven?

So, being one of the created, I take the privilege of
  creating a brand new ancient myth and carve it
    now into the cave wall of my computer screen:

Once upon a way-before time
  and way-before space, nothing existed
    except the Void which was void of everything.

There was no there there and no
  before or after or even anyone
    to worry about all that, but still

even though nothing existed, there was and had
   always been potentiality and if there is
      potentiality something sometime will happen.

It is law.

And so the potentiality discovered itself
   and still there was no thing in the Void
      but now there was thought in the Void

and the potentiality thought that it was two
   which also we do, and we will describe them
      as Feminine and Masculine.

That thought brought yearning and they
   yearned not to be alone and thus
      desire was born and movement began.

The two found that the magnetism was
   delicious and inevitable and felt like life
      though who knew what that was.

Movement accelerated and closer they came
   pulled by irresistible passion, the original
      and exquisite falling in love.

They met and their meeting was an
   explosion of ecstasy noted in history
      as the Big Bang

which produced time and space and matter
  and the planets, moons, stars, galaxies and living
    beings that swim and slither and fly and walk.

The Divine Feminine and the Divine Masculine
  became One God over the vast universe
    their Love had created.

And in that universe the Divine Two
  worshipped each other without ceasing and
    could not stop smiling

and invited their children into
  the potentiality of their own stories
    their own unique and joyful yearnings

and to the inexpressible feast of being in love.

Toward Zion

You can pick up a shovel and dig
  across the entire acreage of patriarchy

and you will not find one gold nugget
  not one buried treasure
    not one hidden spring.

This is a brown and barren land.

It is good for one thing
  purposed well by history:
    to travel over by foot

women and men together
  arms around each other
    walking, dancing, hurrying

following the scent of milk and honey
  toward the promised land of partnership

a Zion discerned in the distance by the joyful
  duet of the shofar and the tambourine
    and then drawing close enough to see

the everywhere
  of irrepressible green.

First Thought of Me

Before the egg and the sperm
   there was a conception.

In the vibration
   that we call heaven
      God had a conversation.

Who are you thinking, my dear?
He said.

Not sure yet,
She said.
Kind of fuzzy. And slow.
This one is hard to conceive of.

Probably a poet,
He said.
That would be nice.
Too many businessmen zipping around.

A poet!
She repeated.
What a concept!
Let me think.

Pregnant pause.

Ah! Yes! She's splendid!
Odd, but splendid!

Do you love her?

Oh, yes!

God laughed
   and the conception
      was complete.

Power

When she learned that
   she didn't have to plug into
      someone or something

like a toaster into a wall

when she learned that she
   was a windmill and had only to
      raise her arms

to catch the universal whisper
   and turn

            turn

                  turn

she moved
   oh, she moved

and her dance was a marvel.

Morning Blessing

Heaven's hands are on my head
    Father, Mother blessing me.

Comfort courses down like rain
    Cleansing and caressing me.

Two Images of the One God

After the Sabbath reading of the Holy Book
  grandfather the rabbi looked at
    his two grandchildren and smiled.

Hannah frowned.

"Grandfather," she said, "why is God always Him?
  Why is God not female?"

Grandfather's eyes brightened and he said

"But He *is*!
  If you look for what hides in plain sight
    on these pages, you discover that:

Our God is a mother who conceived us, gave us life
  a God with a womb who cries out with labor pains
    a nursing God who suckles us

a comforting God who gathers her brood under her wings
  a God who defends us like a mother bear
    a God who hovers over her young like an eagle."

Hannah smiled.

Daniel frowned. Then he said
  "So—God is not male?"

Grandfather laughed and replied
  "But She *is*!

Our God is a father who loves and forgives us
  a potter God who forms our clay to good purpose
    a God who is a king in whom we put our trust

a warrior God who will fight for our good
  a God who is a husband, faithful and kind
    a shepherd God who leads us in righteous paths."

The children studied their grandfather the rabbi
  for he often spoke in riddles.

Now his voice became serious and mysterious.

"In the beginning God created us in God's own image.
  God's female image and God's male image together
    manifest the miracle of our God who is One.

And you, my darlings, are beautiful and equal
  images of God!"

Hannah smiled.

Daniel smiled.

Grandfather the rabbi smiled.

And God smiled.

Women Together

You can fall here.

We are a quilt set to catch you
  a quilt of women's hands
    threaded by pain made useful.

With generations of comfort-making
  behind us, we offer this gift

warm as Grandma's feather bed
  sweet as the Heavenly Mother's
    lullaby song.

You can fall here.

Women's hands are strong.

Unpinned

I hope that humans never
  pin down love or God.

Things pinned down
  (like butterflies)
    lose something (like life).

I welcome progress.
  I am grateful for a long life span
    for medicine and computers.

I like knowing that a black hole
  is born from the death of a star

and that the universe has been expanding
  for 13.8 billion years.

But let some mysteries win.

Let love and God be at liberty
  to touch our faces
    with bright wings

and leave wonder in our eyes
  as they rise, rise

from the hand-held pin
  or the hand-held pen

beautiful as a million monarchs
  and free as the space beyond words.

CREDITS

"A Motherless House," was first published in *Women and Authority*, Signature Books, 1992.

"Women Together" (as "Support Group"), "Don's Daughter," "In Celebration of the First Menstruation," "Position," "Matriarchal Blessing," and "Power" were previously published in *Women I Have Known and Been*, Gold Leaf Press, 1992.

"Running Cloud Speaks," "Holy the Marriage Bed," and "Phoebe the Shaker" were adapted from monologues in *Mother Wove the Morning*, Pearson Publishing, 1992.

"Heavenly Mother's Lullaby" (as "Lullaby of the Heavenly Mother") was previously published in *Lullaby Song*, Embryo Music, 1977 (music by Lex de Azevedo).

"Morning Blessing" (as "Blessing") was previously published in *A Widening View*, Bookcraft, 1983, as was an early version of "Unpinned."

Carol Lynn Pearson is an author, performer, and speaker whose first book of poetry, *Beginnings*, sold more than 125,000 copies worldwide. Included among her more than forty books and plays are *The Lesson, Embracing Coincidence,* and her memoir *Goodbye, I Love You.* Her one-woman play, *Mother Wove the Morning,* in which she plays sixteen women throughout history in search of the female face of God, was performed more than 300 times internationally and received an award from Booklist as one of the top twenty-five videos of the year. She has a master of arts in theater, is the mother of four grown children, and lives in Walnut Creek, California. You can visit her at www.carollynnpearson. com.